THE BLACK MASS

OF THE LOVES OF THE INCUBI AND SUCCUBI

By

MONTAGUE SUMMERS

This edition published by Read Books Ltd.
Copyright © 2019 Read Books Ltd.
This book is copyright and may not be
reproduced or copied in any way without
the express permission of the publisher in writing

British Library Cataloguing-in-Publication Data
A catalogue record for this book is available
from the British Library

CONTENTS

Montague Summers 5

OF THE BLACK MASS; AND OF THE LOVES OF
THE INCUBI AND SUCCUBI 7

Montague Summers

Augustus Montague Summers was born in Bristol, England in 1880. He was raised as an evangelical Anglican in a wealthy family, and studied at Clifton College before reading theology at Trinity College, Oxford with the intention of becoming a Church of England priest. In 1905, he graduated with fourth-class honours, and went on to continue his religious training at the Lichfield Theological College. Summers entered his apprenticeship as a curate in the diocese of Bitton near Bristol, but rumours of an interest in Satanism and accusations of sexual misconduct with young boys led to him being cut off; a scandal which dogged him his whole life. Summers joined the growing ranks of English men of letters interested in medievalism and the occult. In 1909, he converted to Catholicism and shortly thereafter he began passing himself off as a Catholic priest, the legitimacy of which was disputed. Around this time, Summers adopted a curious attire which included a sweeping black cape and a silver-topped cane.

Summers eventually managed to make a living as a full-time writer. He was interested in the theatre of the seventeenth century, particularly that of the English Restoration, and was one of the founder members of The Phoenix, a society that performed neglected works of that era. In 1916, he was elected a fellow of the Royal Society of Literature. Summers also produced some important studies of Gothic fiction. However, his interest in the occult never waned, and in 1928, around the time he was acquainted with Aleister Crowley, he published the first English translation of Heinrich Kramer and James Sprenger's *Malleus Maleficarum* ('*The Hammer of Witches*'), a 15th century Latin text on the hunting of witches. Summers then turned to vampires, producing *The Vampire: His Kith and Kin* (1928) and

The Vampire in Europe (1929), and then to werewolves with *The Werewolf* (1933). Summers' work on the occult is known for his unusual, archaic writing style, his intimate style of narration, and his purported belief in the reality of the subjects he treats.

In his day, Summers was a renowned eccentric; *The Times* called him *"in every way a 'character'" and "a throwback to the Middle Ages."* He died at his home in Richmond, Surrey.

OF THE BLACK MASS

AND OF THE LOVES OF
THE INCUBI AND SUCCUBI

They ate the sacrifices of the dead. Yea, they sacrificed their sons and daughters unto devils. Thus were they defiled with their own works, and went a whoring with their own inventions.
—Psalm CVI (Douai CV), 28, 37, 39.

It is so rash and foolish to deny the fact of these horrible connexions between the demon and human beings that in order to maintain such a position you must be prepared obstinately to reject and spurn the most weighty and carefully considered judgements of the acutest and liveliest intellects, of Saints and philosophers alike, nay, you must wage open war upon experience and common sense, whilst at the same time you are fatally exposing your ignorance of the power of the devil and the empery evil spirits can obtain over man.
—Father Peter Thyraeus, S.J.

"Diabolical Mysticism" includes witchcraft, diabolical possession, and the hideous stories of incubi and succubæ.
—Dean Inge.

The essential feature and climax of the Sabbat orgies was the celebration of the devil's liturgy, the Black Mass.

I am of opinion that being present at a Black Mass is to join in the witches' Sabbat, and accordingly the Satanists who perform the Black Mass to-day and all who attend these vile and impious rites are actually holding a Sabbat.

A curious parallel is noted by Dr. Françoise Legey. On the night of the *Achoura*, the tenth day of Ramadan, in order to renew their magic powers, at the bidding of Eblis (the devil) the Moorish sorcerers secretly penetrate into the mosques and pollute the mat of the Imam. They make their ablutions with sour milk and urinate upon the Koran. They also foul the *tafedna*, the reservoirs of warm water in the public baths. They then hold their Sabbat with vile rites in a cemetery.

In 1324 when the Bishop of Ossory was investigating the sorceries of Dame Alice Kyteler of Kilkenny, "in rifling the closet of the ladie, they found a wafer of sacramental bread, having the divels name stamped thereon in stead of Jesus Christ, and a pipe of ointment, wherewith she greased a staffe, upon which she ambled and gallopped through thick and thin." This sacramental bread has been consecrated at a Black Mass, and it was also proved that Dame Alice, a past-mistress of goety, had sacrificed at the cross-ways nine red cocks to her familiar, Robin, son of Art. It may be observed that the sacrifice of a black cock to the demon is not infrequently mentioned in witch-trials.

The Devil's wafer of grotesque shape or impressed with strange characters was often employed by the witches. Gentien le Clerc, condemned at Orleans in 1614, frequented Sabbats, "and he had often seen the devil's priest elevate the host and the chalice, of which both were black." Thomas Boullé and l'abbé Picard were accused by Madeleine Bavent of employing blood-rear hosts at their foul celebrations; in the Mass of St. Secaire the host is triangular with three sharp points, and black. Similar abominations are usual among the Satanists to-day, so the tradition prevails and Dame Alice Kyteler is closely linked with the twentieth century.

The Neapolitan theologian and legist, Paul Grilland, who wrote on sorcery towards the end of the sixteenth century, describes how unconsecrated wafers are inscribed with letters of blood and amorous devices and thus used at Mass, after which they are crumbled or kneaded into a paste and mingled with food or drink which is given as a love comfit or philtre. One wealthy warlock drew blood from his finger and writing therewith certain obscenities on an altar bread bribed a priest to lay it on the altar-stone under the linen cloths, so that Mass was said over it, with the addition of some secret collects and ceremonies. It may be observed that this practice is not unknown to-day. At Rome there were discovered in a prostitute's house two Hosts inscribed with curious uncials in blood, and these wafers the woman confessed she was going to give secretly to a gallant, beloved by a noble lady, who had furnished the charm. Grilland further discusses in detail the celebrations over unconsecrated breads destined for magical purposes, and also how some interpolate the very Canon of the Mass with lewd and wicked prayers to an evil end. In 1460 at a French trial it came to light that a priest seduced by a witch had actually baptized a toad, fed it with the consecrated Host, and allowed his paramour to use it for the destruction of their personal enemies. The abomination of the Black Mass is performed by some apostate or renegade priest who has abandoned himself to the service of evil and is shamefully prominent amongst the congregation of witches. It should be remarked from this fact that it is plain the witches are as profoundly convinced of the doctrines of Transubstantiation, the Totality, Permanence, and Adorableness of the Eucharistic Christ, as is the most orthodox Catholic. Indeed, unless such were the case, their revolt would be empty and meaningless, void at any rate of its material malice.

Gilles de Sillé of the diocese of St. Malo, and above all the Florentine, Antonio Francesco Prelati, who had been ordained by dispensation at an early age in the Cathedral of Pistoia by the Bishop of Arezzo, served as devil's chaplains to Gilles de Rais, and celebrated black masses in the vaults of the Chapel of St. Vincent at the Chateau of Tiffauges, when children were sacrificed in scores to the demon.

At Tiffauges to-day from the lonely broken arches of the

Chapel one may pass through a cellar door into the crypt below, which dates from the eleventh century. Of no great size and low-sprung the solid roof is transversed by heavy yet not ungraceful semicircular arches supported by massy pillars whose capitals are relieved with carved lozenges and croziers. The place is gloomy, and but a wan watery daylight seems to filter in, showing the rough broken floor in one corner of which gapes the naked opening of some oubliette or little well, down which no doubt were thrown the dead bodies of the children whom Prelati offered upon the altar-stone.

One can well picture the scene illumined only by two black candles, reeking of bitumen and pitch, and by the faint flicker of the rushlight set upon the ground. The silence is broken but by the hoarse blasphemy of the acolyte as he responds in a low tone to the hurried mutter of the young priest clad in the strange vestments of his infernal cult, the mock chasuble of murrey, the hue of dank clotted gore, marked with the inverse cross. The sacred words of power are spoken with a sneer. The golden chalice is raised in hideous parody; the keen knife flashes with swift light, a moment more and the fresh blood gushes from the gaping throat of the youth lying fettered there into the sacramental cup, poor blood commingles with the saving Blood of God, and as the film of death closes over the agonizing eyes of his victim the Italian calls aloud upon Apollyon, the prince of darkness, to accept the sacrifice, to manifest himself and show himself gracious unto his faithful worshippers granting their desire.

It was commonly rumoured that Charles IX of France employed an apostate monk to celebrate the eucharist of hell before himself and his intimates. Bodin at any rate describes how he summoned to his presence a condemned sorcerer named Trois-eschelles du Mayne, who was pardoned on condition that he should give the king an ample account of the Sabbat orgies and all the horrid mystery of witchcraft. This the warlock proved very ready to do, and not only vividly painted Satan's bacchanalia in glowing phrase, but had no scruples about naming a large number of those whom he had recognized at these infernal synagogues.

That the assassination of Henri III, the younger brother and successor of Charles IX, was largely the outcome of constant reports which were assiduously circulating throughout the north of France accusing him of Satanism is now fairly well established. The murder of the Cardinal of Lorraine on the 23rd December, 1588, and the subsequent denunciation of the king from a hundred flaming pulpits as a heretic, deposed, excommunicate, had so incensed popular feeling that a' mere mob revolt blazed forth in civil war, but the charges of devil worship determined his death. A contemporary pamphlet of fifteen pages, octavo, published at Paris in 1589 and entitled

> *The Horrid Sorceries of Henry de Valois, and the Oblations which he offered to the Demon in the Wood of Vincennes. Together with an engraving of the figures of two devils in silver gilt to whom he sacrificed*

openly arraigns the monarch's homosexuality and sorceries in terms of sternest condemnation. It is said that in a grove of the forest of Vincennes there were discovered two silver statues of satyrs, curiously gilded, and about four feet high. In his left hand each held a stout club upon which he leaned, in his right was a small bowl of purest shining crystal. Each stood upon a round base, richly wrought, and supported by four feet chased in the baroque fashion. In the crystal bowls were thin grey ashes, as if a handful of unknown herbs or some sort of incense had been burned. What proved more significant than all was that the satyrs had their back turned to a golden cross, some 3 1/2 feet in length, in the midst of which was set a piece of wood, believed to be a Relic of the True Cross.

The enemies of the king created a resounding scandal out of this mysterious discovery, whilst his friends laughed at the whole business, lightly remarking that the two satyrs were nothing more or less than candlesticks of the antique form. To this it was answered that the figures had no sort of pricket to hold a candle, and the fact that they were placed with their backs to the Holy Cross smelt of sorcery. Nor might this be considered an accidental gesture, since the obscenity of the satyrs betrayed them, and if two tapers should be lit to honour the Relic were not angel-bearers or at any rate plain sconces more appropriate and more decent than lewd heathen goat-men?

Yet another contemporary pamphlet *A Sharp Remonstrance addressed to Henri de Valois* gives fantastic stories of schools for necromancy being established at the Louvre, of the celebration of Black Masses, of the invocation of demons, and how the King maintained a familiar, named Terragon, to whose embraces he compelled a public prostitute to submit herself. Whether Henri III dabbled in occult arts or no can only be regarded as "not proven", for it must be remembered that the evidence is violently prejudiced and inimical, and it is well known that at the very time these and other equally ribald pasquils were pouring from the press and rabid accusations of black magic filled the air the prominent Leaguers were attempting the king's death by fashioning his image in wax and piercing it to the heart with long pins and bodkins, whilst scarcely a day went by that they did not call to consultation some astrologer to read the heavens' face for the royal doom or some foul diviner to cast the runes.

Pierre De Lancre describes in some detail the Black Mass as it was celebrated by the witch covens of the Pyrenees at the beginning of the seventeenth century. The demon or the Grand Master vests himself in the usual robes to say Mass, which is to say (one supposes) he wears the amice, alb, girdle, stole, maniple and chasuble. The words are spoken with a thousand glib sneers and mocking accents. The altar was erected on four supports, sometimes under a sheltering tree, at others upon a flat rock or some naturally convenient place. No *Confiteor* was said, and *Alleluia* was strictly avoided, but the officiant who held in his hand a book of which he frequently turned the leaves began to mutter in a low voice prayers, epistle and gospel, so that it was hardly in this respect to be distinguished from the Mass itself. At the Offertory he drew back a little from the altar and on occasion seated himself, whilst the assembly approached in order, kissed his left hand and presented each one a candle. When the Queen of the Sabbat—the witch who ranked first after the Grand Master, the oldest and vilest of the crew—was present she sat on the left of the altar and received the offerings, loaves, eggs, any meat or country produce, and money, so long as the coins were not stamped with a cross. In her hand she held a small flat disc or plate, technically known as the "pax" or "pax-brede". This was engraved with a figure of the demon, which the whole congregation devoutly kissed.

At this point the Grand Master or some warlock appointed for that purpose preached a sermon, haranguing the assembly in a strain of the most rancid blasphemy and inciting them to every crime.

The ceremonies continued, and the Host which was elevated was seen to be round and black, stamped with a figure of the demon in red. The words, *Hoc est enim corpus meum*, were spoken. The chalice was also elevated. The congregation prostrated themselves upon the earth, and with loud clamours adored. A second discourse or sermon was pronounced and then the mock communion followed. All present were given a particle of the Host, and they drank twice of the chalice, a brew so infect, so stinking, so cold that it seemed to freeze the very marrow of their bones. None the less each one was compelled to swallow the nauseous draught however ill they might stomach it. This description appears to point to some potent drug being mingled in Satan's chalice.

It may be remarked that the use of incense at the Black Mass is very rarely noticed, but Silvain Nevillon, a French witch, spoke of a fume which "smelled abominably foul, not sweet and odorous as is the incense burned in churches". At the modern

Black Mass the rough tang of acrid herbs often fills the air, for the Satanists to-day during their hellish liturgy burn in braziers, chafing-dishes and thuribles rue, henbane, deadly nightshade, lumps of resin and rotting leaves, a smoke and stench which, as one of the gang declared, "is fragrant and grateful to the nostrils of our Master." Boguet speaks of the Black Mass as sung by a priest vested in an old and dirty black cope with no cross on it. "And to make Holy Water the Devil urinates in a hole in the ground, and the worshippers are sprinkled with his filthy stale by the celebrant who has a black asperge."

When Louis Gaufridi, the wizard-priest of Accoules (Marseilles) was brought to trial in February, 1611, a tale of almost unheard-of abomination was ripped open, and Madeleine de la Palud described in amplest detail the countless Sabbats she had attended, where Lucifer's lieutenant, the Prince of the Synagogue (in effect Gaufridi himself), was worshipped with divine honours. The Black Mass was said in Satan's name, either by Gaufridi or by some other miserable wretch, when "the Host was really and truly consecrated and offered to the demon", whilst the Precious Blood was sprinkled from the chalice over the vile crew who shouted and yelled: "His Blood be on us, and on our children!"

Horrible as is the story of Madeleine de la Palud it may be paralleled, and is indeed exceeded, by the narrative of Madeleine Bavent, a Franciscan sister of the Third Order, attached to the convent of St. Louis and St. Elizabeth at Louviers, a little old-world Norman town some twenty-six miles from Rouen.

Mathurin Picard, the evil chaplain of the community, a warlock deeply versed in black magic, was wont to celebrate the infernal eucharist in a midnight vault. Around the altar in this den of devils were set great candelabra, and these alone gave the required light. Mass from the "Book of Blasphemy" was said by Picard, by his assistant Thomas Boullé, and by other wizard-priests who often brought with them Hosts and chalices to be fearfully defiled by the coven. The Host used at these celebrations is described as resembling the usual Altar Bread, but of a slightly reddish hue. At the elevation the whole gang shrieked out the vilest profanities. It was customary for all present to communicate at the eucharist of hell. "Every action I saw performed at the Sabbat," says Madeleine Bavent, "was indescribably loathsome."

In addition to the Black Mass other rites took place—processions, renunciations, liturgical cursings and maledictions, the stabbing and lancing with knives of consecrated Hosts, the throttling of little babes who were sacrificed to the demon. On one Good Friday a woman brought her new-born infant to the Sabbat, and it was decided the child should be crucified, which was done under conditions of peculiar horror. Part of the bleeding body was employed to confect their charms, and the rest they buried.

During the reign of Louis XIV a veritable epidemic of sacrilege seemed to rage through Paris, and indeed the investigations conducted by the Lieutenant of Police, Gabriel-Nicolas de la Reynie, let loose such an avalanche of scandal and crime implicating not only persons of low degree but the highest and most powerful names in France that at the last the King in his absolute authority was of necessity compelled to quash the whole business. Poisons had been brewed, Black Masses said, necromancy practised, abortions procured, murders contrived, plots laid for the death of court favourite and political foe, and all these abominations seemed to centre round two figures of the blackest underworld of Paris, the abbé Guibourg and La Voisin.

Catherine Montvoisin—La Voisin as she was commonly called—had long been known to the criminal and the curious as midwife, poisoner, bawd and witch. There was no infamy which might not be purchased in the secret chambers of her house, No. 25 Rue Beauregard. She was assisted in the many branches of her mysterious and obscene profession by numerous satellites and lovers, chief amongst whom Romani, a handsome young Italian boy and an actor of great talent, filled many a curious rôle. The two executioners of Paris, M. Guillaume and M. Larivière, contended for her favours, gallants who could bring her fine presents of the limbs and fat of murderers who had swung on the gibbet or been broken on the wheel, whence she made tall black tapers for her secret ceremonies. A wanton hermaphrodite, exotic and perverse, La Trianon dwelt in that awful house, to which also daily resorted some curious old women, whose calling no one rightly knew, La Gallet, La Lepère, La Joly, La Filastre, La Bosse, La Thomas. As a matter of fact they were one and all, and a score beside, adepts in the art of poisoning and abortionists of no mean skill and practice. A wit called 25 Rue Beauregard "the centre of the city", and it is no exaggeration to say that all Paris from duchess to drab, from marshal to muckman, crowded La Voisin's doors.

The Abbé Guibourg, known among the witches as M. le Prieur, the illegitimate son of Henri de Montmorency, was a man of some seventy years, who is described as tall and heavy-limbed with a malign and sensual face. "He can be compared with no one else," wrote de la Reynie, "for the tale of his poisonings, and his traffic in drugs and witchcraft. He is familiar with every form of villainy, guilty of a large number of horrible crimes and suspected of complicity in many more." It was M. le Prieur who celebrated innumerable Satanic Masses at the instance of Madame de Montespan in order to secure for her supreme power and the eternal fidelity of the King. Even before Louis had separated from de La Vallière the vicar of St.-Séverin, the Abbé Mariette, had been reciting erotic charms over the hearts of two pigeons consecrated during Mass in the names of Louis de Bourbon and Athénais de Montespan, and apparently the spell had succeeded. But Louis was fickle and apt to be promiscuous in his amours, so his love must be fixed on her alone and the aid of the Abbé Guibourg was requested. In the chapel of the Château de Villebousin near Montlhéry, at Saint-Denis, a long black velvet pall was spread over the altar, and upon this the royal mistress laid herself in a state of perfect nudity. Six black candles were lit, the celebrant robed himself in a chasuble thickly embroidered with esoteric characters wrought in silver, the gold paten and chalice were placed upon the naked belly of the living altar to whose warm flesh the horrible old priest pressed his bloated lips each time the rubrics directed him to kiss the place of sacrifice. All was hushed save for the low monotonous murmur of the blasphemous liturgy. The Host was consecrated, and then the Precious Blood. An assistant crept forward bearing an infant in her arms. The child was held over the altar, a sharp swift gash across the neck, a stifled cry, and warm red drops fell into the chalice whilst the full tide streamed upon the white figure beneath. The corpse was handed to La Voisin, who flung it callously into an oven fashioned for that purpose, which glowed white-hot.

It was proved that a regular traffic had been carried on for years with beggar-women and the lowest prostitutes, who sold their children for this purpose. At her trial La Voisin confessed that no less than 2,500 babies had been disposed of in this manner, for the Black Mass was continually being celebrated not only by Guibourg but by other priests. The figures are so startling that some incredulity has been expressed by those who do not know the Paris of Louis XIV, but there appears no reason to doubt the sum. We may bear in mind that a whole pack of venal and utterly unscrupulous midwives was actively at work; that when the impostume of filth and crime was ripe to bursting no less than 319 warrants were issued, whilst there were very many more whose names were suppressed so deeply did they implicate the highest in the land, nay, the very Throne itself; that six and thirty witches, poisoners and abortionists were executed; that 147, Guibourg, Lesage, Romani, De Vanens, and others were sentenced to close confinement in the remotest fortresses; that many, such as the magician Blessis, went to the galleys for life; and many, again, were conducted by the police over the frontier, condemned to perpetual exile. Several persons died in prison, and others again (of noble and unblemished lineage) committed suicide in agonies of shame lest they should be involved, however remotely, or even as witnesses, in such scandalous and abominable proceedings.

Perhaps the most sad circumstance that came to light during the investigation of these orgies of witchcraft was the large number of priests concerned. Not to mention the mere panders and poisoners—and Éliphas Lévi says that Black Magic is "above all the science of poisoning"—amongst those who habitually celebrated the Black Mass were the Abbé Brigallier, almoner to Mlle de Montpensier, who married the Duc de Lauzun; the Abbé Cotton who offered in sacrifice to Satan a child baptized with Holy Oils used in the Sacrament of Extreme Unction, and then strangled, and whose speciality was "La Messe du Saint Esprit", which is said over a piece of goat's skin sprinkled with holy water and which is intended to cure certain illnesses, to induce love or hate, even to conjure up the demon, all of which Dr. Jean-Baptiste Thiers in his great work denounces as a most pestilent superstition, nay, more, he roundly condemns this practice as a "Witch's Mass", and profane in the highest degree; the Abbé Davot, assistant priest at Notre Dame de Bonne-Nouvelle only a few doors from La Voisin's house, whose custom it was to lay under the corporal at Mass a piece of paper inscribed with the name of the person who should be brought to love, or if hated, damned to die, a practice eagerly pursued to-day—if a priest may be found; the Abbé Deshayes, who demanded exorbitant fees for his Black Masses and who was also a most skilful coiner; Father Gabriel, a Capuchin, who with the Abbé Seysson, was wont to say Masses at La Voisin's house over women's afterbirths and children's cauls to confect charms of particular potency; the Abbé Lepreux, a schoolmaster, deep in the most shameful court secrets, who dedicated infants to the demon, and consecrated snakes and toads to mingle with poisons for their greater efficacy; the Abbé Mabile, who celebrated the sacrifice of the Death's Head; the Abbé Maléscot, who had entered into a sort of partnership with the witch and abortionist, La Gallet, for whom he touted with very considerable success; the Abbé Mariette, who whilst still young had been banished from Paris for his sorceries (it is clear that he was only saved from the stake owing to family interest, for he was of a wealthy and good house), but who returned almost openly to place himself at the service of Madame de Montespan; the Abbé Olivier, who consecrated an altar for Black Masses in a brothel; the Abbé Rebours, who said Black Masses on the body of his mistress; the Abbé Tournet, who said Masses in order to kill the child in the womb, and who was in great request among the evil sisterhood. This catalogue of a dozen wizard-priests drawn from the archives of the Bastille could easily be Multiplied four or five times. There was also Jean-Baptiste Sébault, of the diocese of Bourges, who whilst lodging in Paris at the house of a doctor, named Charmillon, seduced Marianne Charmillon, a girl of twenty-two, his host's daughter, and continually brought her to the Black Mass. The Abbé Guignard celebrated a Satanic Mass in a cellar over her body, and was served by Sébault in a state of complete nudity. An aphrodisiac was brewed at this orgy. The Abbé Lemaignan sacrificed young children, and possessed whole sets of rich vestments in which to celebrate the eucharist of hell.

It is only too much to be feared that the evil science of Guibourg and his company was handed down throughout the eighteenth century. The Duc de Richelieu, who was born in 1696 and died at the age of ninety-two in 1788, was much suspected of studying goety and the worst kinds of occult science. It was said that whilst quite a young man he had formed too close an intimacy with an Austrian noble whose tastes lay in the same direction, and whose wealth enabled him to purchase the secrets of those who had known the Abbé Guibourg and had been instructed by him in every dark secret of magic. Two Capuchins, who were his chaplains, celebrated Black Masses, at which the devotees assisted, in the old deserted chapel of a lone country-house. After this the Duke and his friend defiled the Hosts, in the hope that thereon Satan would appear to crown and reward their blasphemy.

Under the Regency, necromancers and wizards and traffickers in Satanic eucharists abounded, for Philippe d'Orléans was notoriously addicted to occultism of every kind. As might be expected there are revolting pictures of the Black Mass in the lewd pages of de Sade. In *Justine* such a Mass celebrated in a cloister is described in filthy detail. When Juliette is initiated into the "Society of the Friends of Crime" the Host and Crucifix are desecrated. Again, a little later, two Satanic orgies are exhibited, when the High Altar is the scene of every defilement. There are other and even more obscene descriptions of the Black Mass in the work, but these it is unnecessary to particularize.

Upon the night of the execution of King Louis XVI, 21st January, 1793, a number of French devil-worshippers formed themselves into a definite society to foster revolution and propagate their cult of evil. The third chief of this organization died at Florence about 1905. He was believed to be nearly a hundred years old. This particular Society of Satanists spread very rapidly into Italy and soon penetrated Germany. A little later it had established itself very secretly in England, and there can be no question that it has proved one of the most potent forces for evil since its very inception. It has developed and flourished exceedingly and flung out its poisonous tentacles in all directions. It would be no exaggeration to say that much of the world's misery and unrest is due to this foul conspiracy against God and humanity.

Nowhere in France during the first half of the nineteenth century was religious life more fervent and more zealous than throughout the diocese of Agen. Under such saintly Bishops as de Bonnac (the first to refuse the constitutional oath of 1792), and Jean Aimé de Levezon de Vezins pious associations, communities and confraternities were warmly encouraged, not the least of these devout fellowships being the Children of Mary founded by Adèle de Trenquelléon and the widow of a physician, Madame Belloc. This latter lady employed a housekeeper, Virginie (whose surname curiously has not been recorded), and to her horror this woman one day revealed to her pious mistress that she was a Satanist of long continuance, the member of an infernal society which had its headquarters under the very shadow of St. Caprasius, the pro-cathedral. Virginie stated that when about twelve years old she had been taken to a house in the city were was an altar dedicated to the devil, at which an aged priest celebrated a Mass of blasphemy during which there occurred a fearful manifestation of corporeal evil. Moreover she was taught that each Communion she must retain the Host in her mouth, and then eject it secretly so that she might bring it to the midnight Sabbats to be horribly profaned by the impious crew, whose necromancies and conjurations were of the vilest and most abominable description. Madame Belloc hastened to call in the assistance of the Abbé Degans, to whom Virginie confessed that she would sometimes attend as many as five or six early Masses in different churches to obtain the Host. Upon her resolution to repent she fell a prey to an unclean spirit which the Abbé Degans expelled with difficulty and after many exorcisms. One curious feature of the case was the continual apports of Hosts, many of which were marked with bloody characters. Much scandal ensued, and an ecclesiastical inquiry followed. Many suspicious circumstances came to light concerning Virginie when she formed a connexion with the pseudo-prophet Eugène Vintras and his followers, in whose private chapel at Tilly-sur-Seulles (as one of the sect, Gozzoli, quite unequivocally testified) the most horrible obscenities were practised during the celebration of sacrilegious eucharists. It is significant that in 1845 Vintras came to England and established himself in London as the Master of a dark and evil cult which has never died.

THE WITCHES' SYNAGOGUE
Goya

Virginie declared that the Grand Master of the Agen Satanists became truly penitent, and made his peace with Heaven. There can be little doubt, however, that many of the latter statements she made were untrue. It is probable that after her first revelations the Satanists so threatened and terrified her that she lied freely to conceal their identities and their rendezvous. That their chapel was never discovered is no occasion for surprise. They very well know how to cover their tracks.

About the same time 1830–1850 a band of devil worshippers were carrying on their foul witchcrafts at Bordeaux, and numberless Hosts were stolen from the churches, especially from Saint-André and Sainte-Eulalie. In 1852 there burst forth a resounding scandal owing to the celebration of Black Masses in Paris by a band of most impious and malevolent Satanists.

To retail the sacrilege of Black Masses down the years would be weary repetition. Suffice that Satanism in every country yet has its votaries and is extensively practised. It is a matter of notoriety that in 1924 two ciboria, containing 100 consecrated Hosts, were carried off by an old woman from Notre Dame in circumstances which clearly indicated that the holy vessels were not the objects of the larceny. In 1895 a particularly revolting instance of defilement of the Host occurred in the Island of Mauritius. Rome, Salerno, Naples, Florence, Lyons, London, York, Brighton, Brussels, Bruges, and many other towns have all suffered from these abominations. In more than one quarter of London—on the northern heights, in a south-west suburb, in the East End, in the City, by the riverside—have the Satanists made a den, a chapel and altar to the demon they worship with rites of the most horrid lewdness and impiety.

It is very well known that the terrible picture of the black mass drawn by Jorris Karl Huysmans in his masterpiece *Là-Bas* (1891) is true in every detail, and all the characters are taken from life, and have indeed been precisely identified. Thus Madame Chantelouve is (in large part at least) Madame Berthe Courrière, and Docre is named by Mons. Léon Deffoux and other authorities as l'abbé Roca, although Mons. Pierre Dufay, whose opinion carries weight, argues that he is rather Canon Van Ecke (or Van Arche), sometime a chaplain of the sanctuary of the Precious Blood at Bruges.

That extraordinary and erratic visionary the Abbé J.-A. Boullan in a letter to Huysmans, dated 10th February, 1890, says: "Amongst ecclesiastics Satanism is more widely practised and ardently pursued than even in the Middle Ages. It is to be found at Rome; and above all at Paris, Lyons, and Châlons, so far as France is concerned; in Belgium Bruges is their headquarters." Perhaps it should not be forgotten that the orthodoxy of Boullan himself was more than suspect, and whilst there was much open gossip of strange masses by which evil charms and enchantments were dissolved,—the Eucharist of Glory,—there were also darker hints which pointed to plain Satanism. Boullan asserted that he employed White Magic; his opponents—and he had many enemies—declared that he was an adept in Black Magic.

In May, 1895, when the legal representatives of the Borghese family visited the Palazzo Borghese, which had been rented for some time in separate floors or suites, they found some difficulty in obtaining admission to certain apartments on the first floor, the occupant of which seemed unaware that the lease was about to expire. By virtue of the terms of the agreement, however, he was obliged to allow them to inspect the premises to see if any structural repairs or alterations were necessary, as Prince Scipione Borghese, who was about to be married, intended immediately to take up his residence in the ancestral home with his bride. One door the tenant obstinately refused to unlock, and when pressed he betrayed the greatest confusion. The agents finally pointed out that they were within their rights to employ actual force, and that if access was longer denied they would not hesitate to do so forthwith. When the keys had been produced, the cause of the reluctance was soon plain. The room within was inscribed with the words *Templum Palladicum*. The walls were hung all round from ceiling to floor with heavy curtains of silk damask, scarlet and black, excluding the light; at the further end there stretched a large tapestry upon which was woven in more than life-size a figure of Lucifer, colossal, triumphant, dominating the whole. Exactly beneath an altar had been built, amply furnished for the liturgy of hell; candles, vessels, rituals, missal, nothing was lacking. Cushioned prie-dieus and luxurious chairs, crimson and gold, were set in order for the assistants; the chamber being lit by electricity, fantastically arrayed so as to glare from an enormous human eye. The visitors soon quitted the accursed spot, the scene of devil-worship and blasphemy, nor had they any desire more nearly to examine the appointments of this infernal chapel.

A writer of authority has said: "Turning to English accounts, little or nothing of the Black Mass is to be traced," and we find this echoed more than once. The point of the matter lies here. In 1559 Queen Elizabeth initiated her religious settlement by the enactment of Penal Laws, which in a very few years were greatly increased in severity, and since the Act of Uniformity of this year was designed to compel the use of the Anglican Book of Common Prayer it punished by deprivation and imprisonment all clerics who followed any other service. A little later the Mass was prohibited, and in effect the punishment for saying Mass was death. Even in the reign of George III, in 1767, upon the delation of a common informer, the Rev. Mr. Maloney was tried at Croydon for having said Mass and condemned to perpetual imprisonment, but after three or four years the Government commuted the sentence to perpetual banishment. In 1769 the Hon. James Talbot, a brother of the fourteenth Earl of Shrewsbury, and Bishop of Birtha, was tried for his life at the Old Bailey and only escaped owing to a conflict of evidence as the informers obviously did not know what a Mass was and it was urged that the Bishop might have been conducting some other service. The famous Lord Mansfield utilized every technicality and loophole (not to say quibble) of the law to prevent the conviction of priests accused of saying Mass. One point he was wont to urge turned on the fact that the Protestant informers could not be aware in what a Mass consisted and that even if a man were in vestments at an altar using certain ceremonies this might not be the Mass. At any rate it is clear that in Protestant England the Mass had no place, although in certain villages the tradition of the sanctity of the Sacrifice and its mysterious power lingered until the very time of the Oxford Movement. It can, however, be clearly shown, both in England and in Scotland, that the witches celebrated a mock-sacrament.

Before the upheaval under Henry VIII the Black Mass was certainly known in the British Isles. In the twelfth century Gerald de Barry laments those wizard-priests who corrupt the very Sacrament of the Altar to black magic by celebrating Masses over wax images in order to lay a spell on some person, as also others who sing a Solemn Requiem ten times and apply it to some living man that he may die on the tenth day or very soon after, and go down to the tomb. In 1286 an apostate monk, a Cistercian of Rievaulx Abbey, Godfrey Darel, was commonly defamed as a celebrant of Black Masses, and reported to the Archbishop of York.

There is very definite evidence for a mock-sacrament in Scotland as late as the end of the seventeenth century. In August, 1678, the devil convened "a great meeting of witches in Lothian", where amongst others appeared a hideous figure who had once been admitted to the ministry, and had served the parish of Crichton, about six miles from Dalkeith. This warlock parson, Mr. Gideon Penman, was of notoriously evil life and stood in high favour with the devil who spoke of him as "Mr. Gideon, my chaplain". He had turned under the devil a preacher of hellish sermons, for he was reputed very eloquent in the pulpit. In mockery of Christ and His holy ordinance of the Sacrament of His Supper, the devil gave a sacrament to the witches, bidding them eat it, and to drink in remembrance of himself. The villain, Penman, used very readily to assist Satan in these ceremonies, and in preaching. Lord Fountainhall, the famous Scottish lawyer (who was incidentally an extreme Protestant), when describing the same assembly of witches says that the Devil "adventured to give them the communion or holy sacrament, the bread was like wafers, the drink was sometimes blood, sometimes black moss-water. He preached, and most blasphemously".

In New England we find the same tradition of what may be termed the Protestant equivalent of a black mass. The Rev.

George Burroughs, a pastor at Wells, Maine, and Grand Master of the coven, preached to the witches at their meetings, "and there they had a Sacrament" with a woman, Martha Carrier, as Deacon. One member of the gang confessed how "the Witches had a *Sacrament* that day at an house in the Village, and they had *Red Bread* and *Red Drink*". According to Madeleine Bavent the Host at the Mass of blasphemies was red, and there are many references to the Red Drink in the chalice with which the Abbé Guibourg even mingled blood. At Salem the traditional rites of this foul travesty of worship were strictly observed, and these practices must have been carefully handed down and exactly taught to the New England representatives of the witch society.

During the reign of George I the riots of the "Hell-Fire Clubs", which were simply Sabbats of Satanists, had grown to such a height that in 1721 a proclamation was issued for the suppression of "certain scandalous Clubs or Societies of young persons who meet together, and in the most impious and blasphemous manner insult the most sacred principles of our Holy Religion, affront Almighty God Himself, and corrupt the minds and morals of one another". The inquiry was strict, and for a time these Clubs or covens were driven underground. Generally they met in the lowest taverns, where the Satanists of to-day are often wont to forgather to celebrate the Black Mass.

In 1745 the well-known wit, George Selwyn, was sent down from Oxford for celebrating (or at least participating in—the details are not clear) a mock-communion. A terrific scandal ensued, which Selwyn's friend attempted to meet by swearing that the whole business was but a drunken orgy. It is pretty plain, however, that there was a good more in it than that, and the fact that we find Selwyn enrolled a member of the "Monks of Medmenham" is doubly significant.

Medmenham Abbey a Cistercian foundation, is near Marlow, Bucks, on the banks of the River Thames. It was occupied by a notorious profligate, Sir Francis Dashwood, who having converted it into a most luxurious retreat, built or restored a chapel on the model he had seen of the monasteries in France and Italy, and in 1732 here inaugurated "the Order of St. Francis", so dubbed after his own name, also termed "the Franciscans" or "the Franciscan Monks". (It may be remarked that there is an inexactitude here. A Franciscan is a friar, and cannot be a monk.) It seems that only later was this Society known as the "Hell-Fire Club". The original number of members, besides the Superior, was twelve—a witch's coven, and each was baptized with the name of an apostle. It is hardly necessary to give the list in full, more especially as from time to time the numbers varied, but many of the "Order" were in their day famous and influential names, as for example John Wilkes, Charles Churchill, Paul Whitehead, Robert Lloyd, the Earl of Sandwich, George Bubb-Dodington, and Selwyn. A certain young Sir John d'Aubrey also attended the secret meetings. The "monks" or rather Satanists met twice a year for the space of a week. "The cellars were stored with the choicest wines; the larders with the delicacies of every climate; and the *cells* were fitted up, for all the purposes of lasciviousness, for which proper objects were also provided."

There were novices, whose probationary office "was to attend upon their superiours in the celebration of their mysteries, which were all performed in the chapel of the monastery, when no other servants were ever permitted to enter, on the most common occasion, as the very *decorations* of it would in a great measure have betrayed their secrets". The various members of this company were bound to secrecy by oaths and imprecations, since "so outrageous an insult upon the laws was liable to punishment from the secular power".

The initiate clad in a robe of white linen was led to the Chapel at the tolling of a bell, and when at his knock the door opened to the sound of soft and solemn music he had to advance to the communion rails and there make a profession of his principles "nearly in the words, but with the most gross perversion of the sense of the articles of faith of the religion established in the country". The brotherhood knelt round the altar whilst the superior repeated a prayer in the same strain and manner with the *profession* of the candidate *to the Being whom they served*. The novice was elected with mimic ceremonial, and next in a manner not proper to be described, followed their eucharist, every most sacred rite and observance of Religion being profaned, and all the prayers and hymns of praise appointed for the worship of the Deity burlesqued by a perversion to the horrid occasion.

Little wonder that "a formal story was propagated over the whole country, that the end of their meeting was to worship the Devil, to whom this chapel was dedicated, and who had *often* been seen among them, in variety of shapes".

The truth had leaked out, for it is plain from this contemporary account that the Monks of Medmenham were Satanists, who at their Sabbats carried on and perpetuated the foul and blasphemous traditions of the witch.

I have been quoting from Charles Johnstone's key-novel "*Chrysal*: or the Adventures of a Guinea, wherein are exhibited Views of several striking Scenes with Curious and interesting Anecdotes, of the most Noted Persons in every Rank of Life, whose Hands it passed through, in America, England, Holland, Germany, and Portugal", 1760–65. Johnstone in this remarkable book has painted contemporary life with unflinching exactness, and it is certain that either in some way he managed to be present at the mysteries of Medmenham, or else he gained most detailed information from one of the members of that horrid society.

About the middle of the eighteenth century, on the borderland of Germany and the Low Countries, the devil-worshippers joined themselves into a body, a vast secret organization called "Buxen". This grew to be a most formidable gang, terrorizing the whole of the Limburg district and the province of Treves, until a state of appalling anarchy ensued. The custom of the Buxen was to meet after nightfall in some lonely spot and to commence proceedings by the celebration of the Black Mass when Hosts, stolen from the tabernacle were foully desecrated. This was the time for the initiation of recruits. It is said that their obscene ceremonies were generally conducted in one of three ruined sanctuaries, the church of St. Rose near Sittardt, the oratory of St. Leonard hard by Roldyck, and a haunted chapel at Oermond on the Meuse. Afterwards, hideously masqued and disguised, they sallied forth—sometimes to the number of two or three hundred—and raided farms, small holdings, country houses, even attacking villages. If they passed a church on the way they invariably burst open the doors, robbed the tabernacle, and gutted the whole building leaving it in flames. A veritable reign of terror ruled, for so carefully was the secret of membership guarded that no man knew whether his neighbour, nay, his brother or his son might not be a Bux. Any attempt at resistance, any suspicion of treachery, met with the most terrible reprisals. The society was only broken up and crushed after the sternest measures had been taken, a permanent gallows being set up in many places, and some hamlets having two gibbets apiece. Leopold Leeuwerk, dubbed their chaplain, a Satanist who had offered hundreds of Black Masses to the demon, was caught at last, whilst another of their leaders was hanged in 1772 on the moor of Graed, and a few years later the Buxen had come to an end.

Closely connected with the Black Mass of the Satanists and a plain survival from the Middle Ages is that grim superstition of the Gascon peasant, the Mass of St. Sécaire. Few priests know the awful ritual, and of those who are learned in such dark lore fewer yet would dare to perform the monstrous ceremonies and utter the prayer of blasphemy. No confessor, no bishop, not even the Archbishop of Auch, may shrive the celebrant; he can only be absolved at Rome by the Holy Father himself. The Mass is said upon a broken and desecrated altar in some ruined or deserted church where owls hoot and mope and bats flit through the crumbling windows, where toads spit their venom upon the sacred stone. The priest must make his way thither late attended only by an acolyte of impure and evil life. At the first stroke of eleven he begins; the liturgy of hell is mumbled backward, the canon said with a mow and a sneer; he ends just as midnight tolls. The Host is triangular, with three sharp points and black. No wine is consecrated but foul brackish water drawn from a well wherein has been cast the body of an unbaptized babe. The holy sign of the cross is made with the left foot upon the ground. And the man for whom that mass is said will slowly pine away, nor doctor's skill nor physic will avail him aught, but he will suffer, and dwindle, and surely drop into the grave.

When the blasphemous liturgy of the Sabbat was done all present gave themselves up to the most promiscuous debauchery without respect of age, dignity, relationship, or sex. There is no obscenity, says Boguet, which is not practised and eagerly pursued in these assemblies. It is true that the sworn confessions of such witches as Madeleine de la Palud and Madeleine Bavent reveal a veritable abysm of turpitude. Gentien le Clerc, a young Satanist of Orleans, whose mother presented him to the devil when he was but three years old, related how he had assisted at innumerable Sabbats held in a meadow near, or sometimes even in the very market square of Olivet, a village on the left bank of the Loiret, about two and a half miles from Orleans.

The ceremony commenced with an asperges of filthy water or even urine. After this the Devil (the Grand Master) celebrated the Mass. He wore a chasuble of the usual form but embroidered with a broken cross, and after he had elevated the Host and the Chalice, both of which were black, he turned his back to the altar in contempt, as is done in the Satanists' liturgy to-day. The infamous Marie de Sains spoke of a diabolical litany, which commenced—

> Lucifer, miserere nobis,
> Belzebuth, miserere nobis.

The Mass was read from a great book, which seemed to have scarlet letters on the white vellum, and some pages of which appeared all black. It had a rough, furry cover as though made of a wild beast's pelt. The pax was given in the accustomed place, but all present kissed some obscene or grotesque object. After this was done, Gentien avowed that the worshippers, one and all, abandoned themselves to a very riot of lust and spintrian pollutions. To accumulate details were superfluous. The same story is told throughout the centuries. In *Chrysal* Johnstone writes how the Monks of Mendenham after their mock communion service sat down to a banquet "at which nothing that the most refined luxury, the most lascivious imagination could suggest to kindle loose desire, and provoke and gratify appetite was wanting both the superiours and the inferiours vying with each other in loose songs and dissertations of such gross lewdness, and daring impiety, as despair may be supposed to dictate to the damn'd". To-day the meetings of Satanists invariably end in unspeakable orgies of filth and the most hideous debauchery.

The learned authors of the *Malleus Maleficarum* write at length *"Concerning Witches who copulate with Devils"*, and it is obvious that there is no question here of animal familiars, but rather of evil intelligences who are, it is believed, able to assume a body of flesh. As Saint Augustine says, it is beyond all doubt proven that certain devils do continually practise this uncleanness, and tempt others to it, which is affirmed by such grave persons and with such confidence that it were impudence to deny it. A whole catena of authorities from the earliest times until the present day might be cited, but the matter may be summed up as by Delrio who writes: "So many sound authors and theologians have upheld this belief that to differ from them is mere obstinacy and foolhardiness; for the Saints, the Fathers and Doctors, and all the wisest writers on philosophy agree upon this matter, the truth of which is furthermore proved by the experience of all ages and people."

Above all sounds the solemn thunder of the Bull of Innocent VIII announcing in no ambiguous phrase: "It has indeed come to our knowledge and deeply grieved are we to hear it that many persons of both sexes, utterly forgetful of their souls' salvation and straying far from the Catholic Faith have (had commerce) with evil spirits, both incubi and succubi."

The incubus (the word derives from post-classical Latin and literally means *one who lies upon* anything) is the demon who assumes a male form, the succubus or succuba (from late Latin, literally meaning *one who lies under* anything, a harlot) is the demon when assuming a female form, and the famous Dominican Charles Réné Billuart in his *Treatise upon the Angelic Hosts* explicitly informs us: "The same evil spirit may serve as a succubus to a man, and as an incubus to a woman."

Commenting upon the passage in the Book of Genesis (vi, 4), "the sons of God came in unto the daughters of men, and they bare children to them," Pope Benedict XIV explains: "This passage has reference to those Demons who are known as incubi and succubi."

Dom Dominic Schram, a celebrated Benedictine theologian, emphatically lays down: "It is certain that—whatever doubters may say—there exist such demons, incubi and succubi. . . . Wherefore the men or women who suffer these impudicities are sinners who either invite demons . . . or who freely consent to demons when the evil spirits tempt them to commit such abominations."

From these great names, and it were an easy matter to quote a hundred more, it will be seen that the Fathers and Saints, and all scholars and theologians of importance affirm the possibility of commerce with incarnate evil intelligences. The question rises and must be briefly answered how demons or familiars, seeing that they are pure spiritual beings, can not only assume human flesh but thus perform the peculiarly carnal acts of coition and generation.

Following the opinion of Guazzo, who is supported not only by Plato, Philo, Josephus, and other ancient writers, but also by St. Augustine, St. Jerome, and the consensus of all theologians, Lodovico Maria Sinistrari, in his famous treatise *Demoniality* answers that the Demon assumes the corpse of another human being, male or female, as the case may be, or else that from a commixture of other materials he shapes for himself a body endowed with motion by means of which it is possible for the evil spirit to have sexual intercourse with human beings. In this latter instance advantage might be taken, no question, of a person in a mediumistic trance or hypnotic sleep. Jacopo de Voragine relates how once when a priest was sorely tempted by a beautiful woman who entered his chamber in a state of nudity he took his stole and threw it round her neck. With a shriek she fell to the ground, and there lay the rotting corpse of a harlot who had been many days dead.

There is yet another explanation which seems equally possible. Can we not look to the phenomena observed in connexion with ectoplasm as an explanation of this? Again and again in materializing séances physical forms which may be touched and freely handled are built up and presently disintegrate in a few moments of time. In a symposium *Survival* Miss Felicia Scatchere relates certain of her own experiences that go far to prove the partial re-materialization of the dead by the utilizing of the material substance and ectoplasmic emanations of the living. Mr. Godfrey Raupert in his *Modern Spiritism* describes in considerable detail how at these experiments and sittings an entire human form "is fully and immediately 'materialized', . . . The solidity and life-likeness of these forms would seem to depend very largely upon the sensitive and the sitters. If the conditions are very favourable they may have all the characteristics of real human beings with all the functions of a human body in full working order. The pulse or the heart may be felt to be beating, and the organs of sight or of speech or of hearing to be acting to perfection. . . . The forms have been known to remain materialized for a considerable time, to have apported flowers and other light articles, to have carried on prolonged and interesting conversations, and to have acted in other respects like ordinary human beings, possessing and operating in an ordinary human body".

Here then we have an ample solution of the activities of the incubi and succubi, and although neither of these explanations precludes the other, I take this latter to be the more general from the fact that the incubus can assume the shape of some person whose embraces the witch may desire. There are many recorded instances of this, and it is alluded to by the dramatist Middleton in his play *The Witch* when Hecate says:—

> What young man can we wish to pleasure us,
> But we enjoy him in an incubus?

Thus when the young gallant Almachildes visits her abode, she exclaims:—

> 'Tis Almachildes—the fresh blood stirs in me—
> The man that I have lusted to enjoy:
> I've had him thrice in incubus already.

That is the early seventeenth century, and at the end of the nineteenth we find that Huysmans in *Là-Bas* introduces the occultist Ledos under the name Gévingey who discusses in some detail the question of incubi and succubi, relating instances which have come under his own knowledge. I do not hesitate to refer to the pages of Huysmans as it is well known that he had deeply studied the whole subject and he has actual documentation for what he relates. The following conversation takes place between Durtal, who is Huysmans himself, and Madame Chantelouve. This demoniacal woman in a scene of closest intimacy cries to her lover: "You must know then that I can possess you when and how I please, in the same way as I have possessed Byron, Baudelaire, Gérard de Nerval, all the men I love . . ." "What can you mean?" "I tell you that I only have to desire their embrace, as you are longing for me at this moment, and then before I fall asleep . . ." "Well, what then?" "You your real self, will—I know it—prove a mere weakling to the Durtal who visits me at nights, whom I adore, and whose burning kisses drive me mad!" He looked at her in amaze. Then in a flash he realized the truth of those foul incubus lusts of which Ledos had spoken.

We have seen that the Grand Master of a district often presided over and directed the Sabbat orgies, and then it was he, an apostate priest, who celebrated the Black Mass. Sometimes also the familiar assigned to a new witch was in the first place and under certain conditions a man, one of the assembly, who either approached her in some infernal disguise or else embraced her without any attempt at concealment of his individuality, some lusty varlet who would afterwards minister to her pleasure. For we must bear in mind that throughout these witch-trials there is often much in the evidence which may be explained by the agency of human beings, not that this essentially meliorates their offences, for the whole band of sorcerers are acting under Satanic inspiration and are the slaves of the devil. At the same time too we meet those connexions and other dark businesses which admit of no explanation save that of the materialization of evil intelligences of power. Detailed and full as is the evidence we possess, it frequently becomes a most difficult matter when we are studying a particular case to decide whether it be an instance of a witch having had actual commerce and communion with the fiend, or whether she was herself cheated by devils, who mocked her, and persuading her to deem herself in overt union with them, thus led the wretch on to misery and death, duped as she was by the father of lies, sold for a delusion and by profitless endeavour in evil.

It is probable too that a witch would sometimes be served by an incubus or succubus as the case might be, and sometimes by another member of the coven. There are, doubtless, also many cases which stand on the border-line, half hallucination, half reality.

The confessions of the pupils who were in the charge of Antoinette Bourignon afford extraordinary details of these matters. They "declared that they had daily carnal Cohabitation with the Devil; that they went to the Sabbaths or Meetings, where they Eat, Drank, Danc'd, and committed other Whoredom and Sensualities". To repeat the several particular accounts were superfluous. One may suffice for the rest, that of a girl, named Bellot, then aged fifteen. She said that her mother had taken her to a Sabbat whilst she was still very young, "and that being a little Wench, this Man-Devil was then a little Boy too, and grew up as she did, having been always her Love, and Caressed her Day and Night." A young sorcerer from Lorraine, Dominic Petrone, was only twelve years old when his mother enticed him into an abominable marriage of this kind, in which he had much delight.

Remy observes that the demons and witches even simulate marriages, and he records the avowals of sorcerers who had been present at such ceremonies. De Lancre describes how at the Sabbats the Devil performs marriages between warlocks and witches, joining their hands with a sneering benediction. Colette Fischer of Mainz acknowledged that it was no unusual thing for witches to wed demons, who (it is related) feign hot jealousy and carefully watch over their spouses. The Rev. John Gaule in his *Select Cases of Conscience touching Witches and Witchcraft*, published in 1646, mentions that the same customs prevailed in England: "Oft times he marries them ere they part, either to himself, or their Familiar, or to one another; and that by the Book of Common Prayer (as a pretender to Witch finding lately told me in the Audience of Many)." The Capuchin, Jacques D'Autun, writing in 1678, has a chapter upon "The horrid blasphemy and beastliness of these mock-marriages which are celebrated at the witches' Sabbat".

Rebecca West, a witch of Lawford, Essex, and the daughter of a witch, related how the devil came to her "as she was going to bed, and told her, he would marry her, and that she could not deny him; she said he kissed her, but was as cold as clay, and married her that night". He promised to be her loving husband, and swore that her enemies were thenceforth his enemies. "Then she promised him to be his obedient wife till death, and to deny God and Christ Jesus." A young sorcerer, Pétrone of Armentières, declared that when he approached a succuba so intensely cold and gelid did she appear that his own limbs seemed frozen and nipped as with arctic snows. Another warlock, Hennezel, acknowledged that he could not accomplish any venereal act with his succuba, Schwartzburg, who was he verily believed hewn from ice. A Suffolk witch, the widow Bush of Barton, said that the Devil, who appeared to her as a dark swarthy youth, "was colder than man." Isobel Gowdie and Janet Breadheid of the Auldearne coven, 1662, both asserted that the Devil was "a meikle, blak, roch man, werie cold; and I fand his nature als cold within me as spring-well-water".

This unnatural physical coldness of the Demon is commented upon again and again by witches at their trials in every country in Europe throughout the centuries. Now ectoplasm is described as being to the touch a cold and viscous mass comparable to contact with a reptile, and it may be that here we have the solution to the whole mystery.

It is extremely significant too as the pages of Boguet, Remy, De Lancre, and many other demonologists show this coupling with the demon was not accomplished without physical pain. Thus Thievenne Paget declared that the act caused her as keen agony as if she had been in travail. Jeanne Bosdeau who was tried by the Parliament of Bordeaux in 1594 said that the demon "had carnal knowledge of her which was with great pain". The Pyrenean witches acknowledged that this fornication with the devil caused them untold sufferings. Temperance Lloyd, a Devonshire witch, confessed that the Devil had carnal knowledge of her body thrice, and always with great pain.

Moreover it is evident from the several accounts of the Sabbat which agree in various countries that the Devil or President of the assembly was wont to have connexion with every one or at least with very many of the women present. The Grand Master and Officer also exercised the right to select first for his own pleasure such witches as he chose, as appears from a passage in De Lancre who writes that after sorcerer and sorceress had been joined in mock marriage by the Devil he first took the bride's maidenhead.

Obviously no one human being could serve so many women, and it follows that use must have been made of an instrument; the artificial phallus was employed. This is quite clear too from the extremely detailed description of the genital organs of the President of the Sabbat given by the Lorraine witches to Nicolas Remy. Nicole Morèle, Claude Fellet, Alexée Drigie, and indeed the whole infernal sisterhood spoke of these as monstrous beyond all conception. It will not escape notice either that the Devil as drawn from the life—for the sketch was doubtless made at the actual performance—on the title-page of Middleton and Rowley's masque *The World tost at Tennis* is abundantly and indeed grotesquely supplied in this respect. He is pictured in exactly similar fashion in more than one old chap-book, whilst a phallus, to which reference is made in the text, was worn by the actor dressed up as the monkey (*Bavian*) in the May-dance scene in Shakespeare and Fletcher's *The Two Noble Kinsmen*. Troops of phallic demons formed a standing characteristic of the old German carnival comedy. Moreover, several of the fantastic types of the Commedia dell'arte in the second decade of the seventeenth century were traditionally equipped in like manner.

The artificial penis was a commonplace among the erotica of ancient civilizations; it was very generally utilized in Egypt, Assyria, India, Mexico, all over the world. It has been found in tombs; frequently was it to be seen as an ex-voto; in a slightly modified form it is yet the favourite mascot of Southern Italy. Often enough they do not even trouble to disguise the thing. It is mentioned by the Greek writers, by Aristophanes, Herodas, and others. Among the Latins it is spoken of by Petronius and Tibullus. It was familiar in the brothels of Byzantium. It was employed by the Galli, priests of Cybele; in the worship of Bacchus; in the debauched ritual of Priapus. A later historian speaks of phallic ceremonies and the use of ithyphalli in the tenth century. "A sterile lust, common in the earliest times," says the *Erotic Glossary of the Latin Tongue*. The Councils, the Fathers, the Doctors of the Church; Clement of Alexandria, Arnobius, Nicetas, Theodoret, Lactantius, the great St. Augustine, and many a prohibition of West and East have spoken of these practices in terms of severest condemnation. It is demonstrable then that artificial methods of coition, common in pagan antiquity, have been unblushingly practised throughout all the ages, as indeed they are at the present day, and that they have been repeatedly, ay and vehemently, banned and reprobated by the voice of the Church, a malison and an injunction which would doubtless recommend them to the favour of the Satanists, whose dark debaucheries of lust take an additional thrill, a new glamour if they can add to obscenity disobedience. Yet we have also to face the fact that there are darker and fouler mysteries still, hideous copulations of hell, which neither human intercourse nor the employ of a mechanical property can explain.

THE DEVIL CHASTISING THE WITCHES
George Cruikshank

It is the universal opinion that children are born of these horrible unions. These are either demoniac monsters or prodigies of wickedness. They are always in some way hideously deformed, although of course the blemish may be concealed from sight. In any case their odious and malignant nature inevitably betrays the fiendish origin. At Toulouse in 1275, Angèle de la Barthe, a hag of some sixty, was condemned for having had intercourse with an evil spirit from which conjunction she brought forth a vilely misshapen creature whom she nourished with the flesh of infants, slain by her or dug up from their graves in remote churchyards. Towards the end of the seventeenth century an Essex witch, Sarah Smith, from her commerce with a familiar "was brought to Bed of a Strange Monster, the Body of it like a Fish with Scales thereon, it had no Legs but a pair of great Claws. . . . Which eat and fed for some time. Which Monster . . . was by Command of the Magistrates knock'd on the Head, and several Surgeons were there to dissect it". Sinistrari gives the names of several persons who made a noise in the world and were shrewdly suspected of being the offspring of the demon and a witch. Thomas Malvenda, a famous Dominican writer, says that children thus begotten are often tall, very hardy and bloodily bold, arrogant beyond words, and desperately wicked. Both Malvenda and St. Robert Bellarmine hold that Antichrist will be the progeny of a demon and a witch. Others indeed have it that Antichrist will be the Devil in the flesh in awful mockery of the Incarnation. Be that as it may, the appalling wickedness, the power and infinite capacity for evil of certain prominent figures to-day can only be explained if we realize that such must verily be the children of Satan and witches.

    A candid consideration will show that for every detail of the Sabbat, however fantastically presented and exaggerated in the witch-trials of so many centuries, there is amplest warrant and unimpeachable evidence. There is some hallucination no doubt; there is lurid imagination, and coarse vanity which paints the colours thick; but there is a solid stratum of fact, and very terrible fact throughout. And to-day the Satanist is as tirelessly active in our midst as ever he was in bygone ages. Nay, actually the Devil is massing his forces on every side.

Generally the Sabbat orgies lasted till cock-crow, before which time none of the assembly was suffered to withdraw. It is true that in the avowal of Louis Gaufridi, executed at Aix in 1610, he speaks of remaining at the Sabbat two or three hours, just as he felt inclined, but this seems altogether exceptional, and he was moreover the Grand Master of the coven. That the crowing of a cock dissolves enchantments is a tradition of extremest antiquity. The Jews believed that the clapping of a cock's wings will render the power of demons ineffectual and dissolve all magic spells. The poet Prudentius sang: "They say that the foul night-wandering spirits, who rejoice in dunnest night, at the crowing of the cock tremble and scatter in sore dismay." In the time of St. Benedict Matins and Lauds were recited at dawn, and were often known as *Gallicinium*, Cock-crow. The rites of Satan ceased when the Office of Holy Church began.

At the hour of the Nativity, that most blessed time, the cocks crew all night long. A cock crew lustily at the Resurrection. A witch named Babilla Latoma confessed to Nicolas Remy that the cock was the most hateful of all birds to sorcerers. Johann Bulmer and his wife Desirée, who belonged to a coven of Le Mans district, said that the synagogue of sorcerers was usually disbanded by the President and the familiars proclaiming: "Ho! Speed all and away—away! For the cocks begin to crow!"

The sound of bells also is most detested by the hellish crew, and Bishop Binsfeld in a fine passage compares the music of church bells to the hoisting of the royal standard of our King. Not only can they subdue tempests but they put to instant flight devils and witches, they breathe benediction and peace. It is recorded by an Italian writer that on a certain occasion when the debauchery of the Sabbat had been prolonged the horrid crew were surprised to hear the Angelus ringing out its early salutation to the Virgin Mother from a village steeple hard by. The demons fled howling and disappeared with a most noisome stench abandoning their besotted worshippers to fare as best they might. Bishop Peter

Binsfeld says that the charm was broken, the glamour dissipated, and the Sabbat vanished if one pronounced with devotion the Sacred Names of Jesus or Mary.

The Sabbat ends. As the dawn breaks the unhallowed crew separate in haste, and hurry each one on his way homewards, pale, weary, and haggard after the night of taut hysteria, of frenzied evil, hate, and vilest excess.

The cock crows; the Sabbat ends; the sorcerers scatter and flee away.

www.ingramcontent.com/pod-product-compliance
Lightning Source LLC
Chambersburg PA
CBHW030124170426
43198CB00009B/728